THE POWER OF
Hell Naw!

VENUS CHANDLER

© Copyright 2024

IBG Publications, Inc.

VENUS CHANDLER

Published by I.B.G. Publications, LLC, a Power to Wealth Company

Web Address: WWW.IBGPublications.Com

admin@IBGPublications.Com / 904-419-9810

Copyright, 2024 by Venus Chandler

IBG Publications, Inc., Jacksonville, FL

ISBN: 978-1-956266-79-5

Chandler, Venus
The Power Of Hell Naw

All rights reserved. This book or its parts may not be reproduced in any form, stored in a retrieval system, or transmitted in any form, by any means-electronic, mechanical, photocopy, recording or otherwise, without prior written permission of the publisher or author, except as provided by the United States of America Copyright law.

Printed in the United States of America.

THE POWER OF Hell Naw!

Dedication

This book is dedicated to:
"To My Mother, Who Carried the World"

To My Mom

This is for you, Mom. You carried the weight of the world on your shoulders, always giving without hesitation, never knowing how to say 'no.' You gave so much of yourself, often at the cost of your own needs and peace. Now, I see how much you carried, how much you endured, always trying to keep everything and everyone afloat.

I wish you could have felt the freedom to set boundaries, to guard your heart as fiercely as you loved others. But in your quiet strength, you taught me the beauty of compassion, resilience, and the importance of knowing when to lay burdens down. I honor your life by learning what you couldn't, and I carry your love with me every day. You are forever in my heart.

VENUS CHANDLER

To Myself

This book is dedicated to the woman I've become—through every trial, every heartbreak, and every victory. It's a testament to my journey: a journey of fighting for peace, strength, love, and forgiveness, while learning the sacred art of boundaries. I've discovered the true power of saying 'Hell No'—not in anger, but out of love for myself and respect for my own worth. This is my declaration: I will continue to stand firm, protect my peace, and walk in the strength that comes from truly knowing who I am.

To Aunt Ivy

This book is also dedicated to you, Aunt Ivy. Thank you for being my rock through life's rough valleys. You held my hand, guided me with wisdom, and taught me the power of setting boundaries. You showed me that saying 'no' is an act of self-love and strength. Thank you for being my teacher, my friend, and my counselor. Your guidance has shaped the woman I am today, and I am forever grateful for your love and support.

To My Spiritual Sister: Audrea V. Abraham.

My dearest friend and spiritual sister, thank you for never leaving my side, for always believing in me, and for pushing me to see the truth of who I am. You helped me realize that the power I was searching for has always been within me. You taught me how to set boundaries, to say 'no' when needed, and to embrace the beauty of being comfortable in my own skin. You reminded me to put myself first and to stop sacrificing so much of myself for others. Your unwavering support has been a true gift, and I am forever grateful.

VENUS CHANDLER

THE POWER OF *Hell Naw!*

TABLE OF CONTENTS

DEDICATION... 3
INTRODUCTION... 9

The Power Of Hell Naw!............................... 15

Silent No More!.. 25

Boundaries... 37

The Choice Is Yours..................................... 47

The Big F... 55

Declutter.. 65

Owning Your Crap.. 71

Navigating Forward...................................... 77

About The Author.. 83
More Books by the Author........................... 87

*"We delight in the beauty of the **butterfly**, but rarely admit the changes it has gone through to achieve that beauty."*

Dr. Maya Angelou

INTRODUCTION

VENUS CHANDLER

After completing my first book, *A Silent Scream: My Story, My Truth*, I felt a sense of relief. It was as though I had finally purged all the hurt, pain, disappointments, and poor life choices. A major shift had taken place in my life, and I believed I could finally move forward. I gave myself permission to no longer let the past haunt me. I was able to forgive myself and feel true happiness for the first time.

However, that feeling didn't last long. Some people were deeply upset with me for sharing my truth. When my book was first published, I was paralyzed with guilt, feeling as though I had hurt the people I loved and cherished. I didn't know how to handle it. I cried for days, stopped eating, stayed in the dark, called out of work, and sank into a deep depression.

In desperation, I decided to pull the book from the market, and cancel all my book signings; I thought this would make everything better. But I was wrong—very, very wrong.

THE POWER OF Hell Naw!

Instead of healing the situation, my truth damaged relationships and made people resent me, nearly to the point of hatred. Before I knew it, I was being revictimized, trapped in the same emotional hell I thought I had escaped forever.

One morning, God placed it on my heart that He had given me my purpose, but I had thrown it right back in His face. He told me that this path would be painful and there would be separation. At first, I didn't fully understand, but then He led me to a book I had purchased months earlier, *Spirit Check* by Michelle Collins. I hadn't realized it at the time, but God had been preparing me, knowing exactly what I needed, even when I didn't.

When I opened the book and read the chapter titled "Spirit of Intimidation," my life was forever changed. It was as though God was speaking directly to me. If you're struggling, this book is a "must-read"—it has the power to transform your life too.

VENUS CHANDLER

My book, *A Silent Scream: My Story, My Truth*, was never written to hurt anyone. I wrote it because I was dying inside. I was so deeply depressed and couldn't find a way to move beyond my past. I had begun contemplating suicide over and over. I was miserable, trapped in pain, and didn't know how to free myself from it. Writing that book was my way of trying to survive.

I sincerely apologize to anyone who was hurt by me writing about my truth. It was never my intention to cause pain. I simply wanted to live, and I knew that sharing my story was the path to make that happen. I wanted to live and not die.

Writing about my childhood traumas helped me find my voice, which in turn gave me my power back. Through this, I discovered my true purpose in life. I must say, finding my voice, reclaiming my power, and stepping into my purpose feels incredible. I've made a promise to myself and to God that I will never let anyone take that away from me again.

THE POWER OF *Hell Naw!*

After completing my first book, my life changed dramatically. I began setting boundaries, saying "no," and asking for what I truly wanted. As I made these changes, people started asking me, *"How did you do it? How did you change your life? How did you take back your power and find your purpose?"*

With so many people asking these questions, I realized it was time to write again—this time, to share the steps I took to transform my life. I wanted to provide a guide for others, showing how I was able to accomplish these things.

* * *

Now, let me address something, because I know there will be people asking questions. Questions like, *"Who is she to tell me anything? She's not a therapist, an evangelist, a pastor, or a preacher."*

No, I am none of those things.

But let me tell you who I *am*. I am ***Venus***, a survivor of childhood trauma—trauma that involved physical, mental, verbal, and sexual abuse. I escaped hell, and that makes me an expert in surviving childhood trauma. I also know how to help others escape their own hells, the ones they're trapped in because of their past.

In the following chapters, I'll share how I changed my life. I'm not saying this is the only way, or even the best way, but it's the formula that worked for me. And maybe, just maybe, it will work for you too.

Take the journey with me in this powerful book and watch yourself reclaim your power and your voice. No one should ever be held captive in a prison of trauma or violated boundaries. You have the right to maintain your peace, at any cost. And remember, anything worth having is worth paying for.

Let's take the journey, you're worth it!

THE POWER OF Hell Naw!

VENUS CHANDLER

Here's a few quick questions to ask yourself that come with your power to say, 'Hell Naw!'

- ✓ What does the "Power of Hell Naw" have to do with change?
- ✓ Why is this phrase so powerful?
- ✓ How does it help you to regain control of your life, voice and power?

One of the smallest words in the English language, "No," is also the most powerful. It's a word that will help you grow both personally and professionally. Saying "No" liberates you, while saying "Yes" often commits you to things that may not align with your purpose.

But to say, "no," you must gain an understanding of what your purpose in life is. You cannot impose such boundaries without understanding the "why."

As you continue to journey through this book, I want you to start thinking about what your life purpose is.

THE POWER OF Hell Naw!

Understanding your purpose will help you navigate all the advice and tips I give in this book.

* * *

When I think of the power of "No," I think of the phrase "Hell naw!"—a phrase that embodies strength and conviction. I had no clue how important the word "No" was, what it truly meant, or just how powerful it could be. I didn't even realize I had the right to say "No."

I remember my mom once told me that saying this word is especially hard when it comes to the people you love. She gave me an example: "Venus, when someone stops and asks you, 'Do you know what time it is?' simply say 'No.'" She told me, even if I had a watch on my arm, to still say "No," and nothing more. No explanations. No excuses. Just "No."

I must admit, this was the hardest thing for me to do. It took me years to get it right. But trust me, once I mastered it, I started saying "No" just for the hell of it—to make sure I hadn't lost the ability!

The truth is, other people aren't concerned about your boundaries; they are more interested in how you can serve them. That's why learning to say "No" is crucial. It's a shield that protects your time, energy, and mental health.

> *You will never reach your destination if you stop and throw stones at every dog that barks.*
> ~Winston Churchill

They don't care about your needs; they're only focused on their own. That's life. Too often, we end up saying "yes" to every request because we fear criticism, rejection, or losing a friend. But it's better to say "No" to a request if you're not fully committed, rather than saying "yes" and failing to follow through on your promises.

Many people try to please everyone by saying "yes" all the time, but in doing so, they end up pleasing

THE POWER OF *Hell Naw!*

everyone but themselves. Think about it: every time you say "yes" to something new, you're taking time away from something that truly matters to you.

Saying "No" protects you from distractions, chaos, and external noise, helping you stay focused on your priorities. Remember, turning down a request isn't the same as turning down a person, it's not personal! There's nothing wrong with setting boundaries and protecting your own well-being.

- ✓ Say **'No'** to any relationships which don't make you happy and drain all your positive energy
- ✓ Say 'No' to spending time with people who don't have a clear purpose or positive influence in your life—they are the biggest timewasters.

> *Innovation is saying 'no' to 1,000 things.*
> ~Winston Churchill

Say "No" to new ventures if you're unsure of their potential for long-term success, as they require a great deal of commitment and energy to truly succeed. Focus on what aligns with your goals and values.

- ✓ Say "No" to excessive social networking and instead focus on prioritizing the relationships that are truly meaningful to you. Deepen those connections rather than constantly seeking out new ones.
- ✓ Say "No" to anything that doesn't align with your priorities and concentrate on what truly matters to you.

To make your 'no' effective, start by writing down your goals and what's important in your life. Each time you receive a new request, ask yourself: "Is this important to me?" and "Will this help me achieve my long-term goals, or will it just distract me again?"

THE POWER OF Hell Naw!

In closing this chapter, *The Power of Hell Naw!*, it's clear that there's a force within every person that refuses to settle, compromise, or bow to the things that threaten their inner peace, purpose, and dignity. This power is more than a response, it's a declaration, a boundary, and a commitment to stand firm.

Saying "hell naw" is not just about rejecting what is wrong; it's about boldly affirming what is right, aligning with higher values, and embracing the self-worth and courage to protect what truly matters.

In a world full of pressures, temptations, and challenges, the power of "hell naw" becomes an unshakable defense, an armor that shields one's soul. It's a reminder that true strength often lies in the simple yet profound ability to say "no" to anything that detracts from one's path or purpose. Every time we choose "no" over compromise, we empower ourselves, reinforce our boundaries, and affirm our values.

So, as we step forward, let this power guide decisions, protect boundaries, and ignite courage. This chapter closes but may the power of "hell naw" remain an ever-present strength, helping to steer us away from the pitfalls and toward the promise of a life lived fully, freely, and unapologetically true.

Before we move forward into more of your newfound freedom, take some time to write down 5 instances when you should have said, 'no,' and did not. Then reflect on how you will respond in the future to protect your peace.

1.) _____

_____

_____

2.) _____

_____

_____

THE POWER OF *Hell Naw!*

3.) _____

_____

_____

4.) _____

_____

_____

5.) _____

_____

_____

_____

_____

_____

_____

"Once you're super clear about what exactly you want, you will stop being susceptible to what other people think you should do, and you do only what's really important to YOU."

-Steve Jobs-

SILENT NO MORE!
You Are The Author Of Your Story

VENUS CHANDLER

"There is no greater agony than bearing an untold story inside you."

~Maya Angelou

Telling your story, your truth, is your right. You owe no one an explanation, nor do you need to ask for permission. The only thing you need to do is put people on notice! These are the words that may best describe someone who may be offended by your truth: *"If you wanted a different role in my story, then you should have played a different part in my life."*

May be hard truth, but it is valid, nonetheless.

Everyone has a story to tell, and some of those stories, if left untold, can feel like they are killing you inside. These untold stories can be like a "cancer" growing within, making you sick and draining life out of you. You are the author of your life, and you have the power to write about it as you choose. Whether you publish a book, keep it to yourself, or simply journal, writing is one of the best ways to regain control over your life. It allows you to rewrite your story and shape its outcome on your own terms.

When I started writing my first book, *A Silent Scream: My Story, My Truth*, I was so concerned about who I might hurt by telling my story. This fear weighed on me so heavily that it took years to complete the book.

But in the process, I had a breakdown because I could no longer control the "cancer" growing inside of me; I had to kill it at the root.

This emotional "cancer" had spiraled out of control, taking over my body and mind. Eventually, worrying about hurting others or what they thought no longer mattered—I wanted to live.

Telling my story wasn't easy. In fact, it was the most painful thing I've ever done. I've had children, got tattoos, piercings, and even broken a bone or two, but none of that compared to the pain of telling my truth. Reliving the trauma of molestation, mental, physical, and emotional abuse was excruciating. As I wrote, I started to smell familiar smells, taste things that overpowered my mouth, and feel fear all over again. There were countless times I wanted to quit and allow cancer to grow. But I was determined to survive and telling my story was my own form of chemotherapy.

With the help of my higher power—God—I kept pushing through. I was committed to living, no matter how painful it was to confront my past.

Finally, I completed my book, told my story, and shared my truth. Since doing that, I've regained my life, my power, and my voice.

I am truly stronger than I've ever been in my entire life. For the first time, I am happy, whole, and mentally healthy. With this newfound strength, I'm able to cultivate healthier relationships, make better choices, and make wiser decisions. Most importantly, I'm now able to help others tell their own stories.

I'm not saying all this magically happened the moment I finished writing my book. But what I **am** saying is that it was the beginning. It took a great deal of hard work, self-development, and determination to create real change in my life. Writing my book was a purge, a cleansing of my soul, and through that process, I became "new" in the eyes of God.

I was given a clean slate, a second chance, or a "do over," if you will. With that in mind, I've learned to be very careful about what I allow into my body, mind, and soul from that point forward. I've become fiercely protective of my peace and well-being.

~Be Silent Never Again!

The Consequences Of Hiding Your Truth

Considering being the author of your own story, the importance of standing firm in one's truth is paramount, as failing to do so can have far-reaching consequences on the body, mind, and spirit.

When someone suppresses their truth, they may unknowingly invite toxicity into their life, allowing harmful influences, people, and situations to linger unchecked. Over time, this silence can lead to internalized stress, which affects every dimension of their well-being.

1. **Body**: When a person holds back their truth, the stress and tension often manifest physically. Repressed emotions can lead to chronic stress, which has been linked to various physical ailments such as high blood pressure, digestive issues, headaches, and even compromised immunity. The body becomes a reservoir of unsaid words and unexpressed emotions, slowly deteriorating under the weight of what is left unspoken.

2. **Mind**: Mentally, the refusal to own one's truth can create a breeding ground for self-doubt, anxiety, and confusion. When one ignores their true feelings or convictions, they may feel disconnected from themselves, fostering feelings of frustration and inner conflict. This mental strain often leads to a cycle of overthinking and self-criticism, affecting one's focus, productivity, and overall mental health.

3. **Spirit**: The spirit, at its core, thrives on authenticity and alignment with one's true values and purpose. When someone silences their truth, they disconnect from their essence, creating a void where vitality and purpose should dwell. Spiritually, this disconnection can lead to a sense of emptiness, guilt, or even shame. Over time, the individual may feel unfulfilled, as if they are living a life that isn't truly theirs, missing out on the power and

peace that comes from being unapologetically authentic.

Acknowledging these consequences highlights why standing firm in truth is essential. Saying "hell naw" to compromising one's truth not only protects the body, mind, and spirit from unnecessary harm but also empowers individuals to live boldly, confidently, and healthily. Living authentically is not only a right; it is a pathway to freedom and wholeness, allowing one's light to shine without restriction.

The Benefits Of Sharing Your Truth

Embracing and speaking one's truth is shown to be an act of empowerment that brings profound benefits to the body, mind, and spirit. Owning one's truth allows for freedom, confidence, and alignment with one's deepest values, creating a life that reflects true self-worth and inner peace. Here are some powerful ways that telling your truth can positively impact every dimension of your being:

THE POWER OF Hell Naw!

1. **Body**: When individuals express their truth, they release the stress and tension that comes from holding back. This honesty helps to lower cortisol levels and can improve overall physical health by reducing the risk of stress-related ailments like high blood pressure, muscle tension, and digestive issues. The body relaxes and functions more optimally when it's not holding onto unspoken burdens. Furthermore, telling the truth fosters a sense of confidence and peace, leading to improved sleep, increased energy, and a healthier, more vibrant physical state.

2. **Mind**: Mentally, telling the truth creates clarity, reduces internal conflict, and builds self-respect. When people stand in their truth, they gain mental resilience and a stronger sense of identity, which helps to minimize self-doubt and indecisiveness. The freedom to be honest also cultivates mental clarity and focus,

as one no longer must expend energy on masking or censoring thoughts. Speaking truthfully helps to nurture a mindset of self-acceptance and confidence, empowering one to face challenges with courage and composure.

3. **<u>Spirit:</u>** Spiritually, living in truth aligns one's actions and words with their core values, fostering a deeper connection with their authentic self. This alignment cultivates inner peace, fulfillment, and a sense of purpose, as it allows the spirit to live freely and boldly. Embracing truth strengthens one's sense of integrity and spiritual vitality, making room for joy, creativity, and personal growth. When a person speaks and lives truthfully, they honor their own journey, becoming a light for others who seek to live with similar freedom and authenticity.

THE POWER OF *Hell Naw!*

These benefits underscore why standing in one's truth is a transformative act. Telling the truth is a way of saying "hell naw" to compromising oneself, embracing instead a life of courage, resilience, and self-love. By living authentically, individuals experience greater health, mental peace, and spiritual joy, creating a life that radiates true strength and fulfillment.

VENUS CHANDLER

BOUNDARIES

VENUS CHANDLER

There are many types of boundaries—emotional, physical, personal, and more. But at their core, boundaries all share the same purpose: they are the limits and rules we set for ourselves within relationships.

A person with healthy boundaries can say "no" when necessary, while also being open to intimacy and close connections. Boundaries are not about pushing people away—they exist to protect us! There are ways of telling others what you will and will not tolerate.

> "Daring to set boundaries is about having the courage to love ourselves, even when we risk disappointing others."
> ~Brené Brown

Establishing healthy boundaries in relationships is crucial for personal well-being and the success of the relationship itself. While specific statistics on success rates directly linked to boundary-setting are limited, research indicates that individuals who practice self-control—a key component of setting boundaries—experience more satisfying and enduring relationships.

A study published in the *Journal of Personality and Social Psychology* found that adolescents with higher levels of self-control were more likely to have better intimate relationships 23 years later, which is well into their adulthood. These individuals reported higher relationship satisfaction, less conflict, and improved communication in their relationships.

Additionally, maintaining healthy boundaries can prevent burnout and resentment in relationships. The *Mayo Clinic Health System* emphasizes that setting boundaries is essential for reducing stress and increasing satisfaction in both personal and professional relationships.

While more research is needed to quantify the direct impact of boundary-setting on relationship success rates, existing studies and expert opinions underscore the importance of boundaries in fostering healthy, fulfilling, and lasting relationships.

Before I wrote my first book, I didn't fully understand what boundaries were. I had no idea how to set or enforce them. I didn't realize that boundaries are how you communicate to others what is acceptable in your life. Setting boundaries is a way of showing that you are in control, you set the rules, and you enforce them.

So, how do you use your boundaries?

They start by understanding that you have the right to protect your well-being and set limits in any situation. They empower you to take control of your life, to define what is and isn't okay, and to confidently stand by those choices. **(Source: Psychology Today)**

Here is a mental checklist you can perform when entering new relationships, ensuring you get off to the right start:

THE POWER OF Hell Naw!

1. Know Your Limits

From the beginning, clearly define your intellectual, emotional, physical, and spiritual boundaries with different groups of people, such as strangers, colleagues, friends, family, and intimate partners. Reflect on past experiences where you felt discomfort, anger, resentment, or frustration with someone. Identify behaviors or situations you will no longer tolerate. This self-awareness will help you establish clear boundaries.

2. Be Assertive

Setting boundaries early on is important, but what truly matters is enforcing them. The only way others will know they've crossed your boundaries is if you're direct and assertive with them. Being assertive, especially if you're not used to it, can feel intimidating at first. Start small by addressing manageable situations, and gradually build your assertiveness skills for more significant boundaries.

3. Practice Makes Perfect

When you begin the relationship being assertive, especially if it's new to you, you might fear that others will see you as mean or rude. However, standing firm in your boundaries shows that you value yourself, your needs, and your feelings above the opinions of others. Being assertive doesn't mean being unkind—it means being fair and honest. In the long run, it's kinder to everyone involved; while helping you maintain your peace, dignity, and self-respect.

4. *If All Else Fails, Delete and Ignore*

Begin by voicing your boundaries clearly. Then, if they continue to be crossed, follow through with action. If you've addressed the situation and communicated your needs, it's perfectly okay to step away from individuals, whether family, friends, or ex-partners—if they refuse to respect your boundaries.

Whoever it may be, once you've provided closure on any promises you make, you no longer owe them anything. If you have clearly asserted your boundaries and communicated that someone is not respecting them, it's perfectly okay to ignore further correspondence from that point on. Remind yourself of your own worth and remember that no one has the right to make you feel uncomfortable or take away the personal space you've defined for yourself.

Why must we have boundaries?

(Jane Collingwood)

Setting clear personal boundaries is essential to ensuring that relationships are mutually respectful, supportive, and caring. Boundaries reflect your self-esteem—they establish the limits for what behavior is acceptable from those around you. Without them, people may feel entitled to put you down, make fun of you, or take advantage of your kindness.

Weak boundaries leave you vulnerable, often resulting in being taken for granted or even harmed by others. On the other hand, healthy self-respect fosters boundaries that communicate you deserve to be treated with respect. They protect you from exploitative relationships and help you avoid getting too close to those who don't have your best interests at heart. Reset your boundaries as often as needed and remain consistent in enforcing them.

As we conclude this chapter, here is a checklist to help ensure that you are setting healthy boundaries. After reviewing it, take some time to journal about the people in your life with whom you need to set boundaries, and reflect on why. This quick self-therapy session will help you explore where you are in this process and guide you in moving forward.

<u>Checklist</u>: **How to Create Healthy Boundaries:**

1. *Identify Your Limits*
    - Reflect on what makes you uncomfortable or drains your energy.
    - Consider emotional, physical, and mental boundaries.

2. *Communicate Clearly*

- Use direct, assertive language to express your needs.
- Keep it simple: "I'm not comfortable with that" or "I need some space."

3. Be Consistent

- Stick to your boundaries once they're set. Consistency builds respect.

4. Practice Self-Awareness

- Check in with yourself regularly. Adjust boundaries if needed.

5. Start Small

- Set boundaries in low-risk situations first to build confidence.

6. Be Prepared for Resistance

- Understand that others may push back. Stand firm and repeat your boundaries calmly.

7. *Prioritize Self-Care*

- Remember that boundaries are about protecting your well-being, not pleasing others.

8. *Recognize Toxic Patterns*

- Identify relationships where boundaries are ignored or violated and take steps to protect yourself.

9. *Seek Support*

- Reach out to a therapist or trusted friend for advice or reinforcement.

10. *Stay Empowered*

- Reinforce that saying "no" is not selfish—it's necessary for your health and happiness.

Making the choice to change, be RADICAL!

THE CHOICE IS ALL YOURS

The 3 C's of Life:

1) Choices
2) Chances
3) Changes

"You must make a choice to take a chance, or your life will never change."

-Coach Venus Chandler

The decision to change happens in a single moment; it's not a gradual process over time. Many people believe that change is something you ease into, but the decision to change occurs in an instant.

When something is considered extreme or unlike anything that came before, it's called radical. In everyday terms, a radical person is someone with very extreme views. Similarly, a radical change or flaw is one that is fundamental and transformative.

THE POWER OF *Hell Naw!*

To create real change in your life, you must become radical. You must make it clear that this transformation is permanent, and if others can't accept it, they can exit stage left.

> *"Progress is impossible without change, and those who cannot change their minds cannot change anything."*
> ~George Bernard Shaw

I guess you could call me radical because I became an extremist in my life. I adopted bold, extreme views and stopped caring about what people thought of me.

I made a radical change, and when I did, people thought I was insane. Someone even told me I was a very sick person.

They said, "Your mom was a very sick woman, so you must be sick like she was."

By "sick," they meant mentally unstable. But let me be clear—I am not mentally unstable. At least, not anymore. I was just fed up with being treated like crap.

VENUS CHANDLER

People have a strange way of thriving off your misery. Believe it or not, there's a word for this—it's called *schadenfreude*. It's the experience of pleasure or satisfaction from seeing someone else suffer, fail, or be humiliated.

But I refuse to wear the "mentally ill" label any longer! I wasn't mentally ill—I was lost. I didn't have anyone to guide me or show me the way. I was confused, and all I knew was that I wanted the pain to stop.

People treated me terribly, including family, friends, husbands, and colleagues. I was sick and tired of people taking my love and kindness for weakness. I was tired of being used. People saw how desperate I was for love and acceptance, and they preyed on me, draining me dry. And when I say "people," it was mostly those closest to me who took advantage.

Change your mind, and you will change your life. Nothing will shift in your life until you do. Life is short- too short to keep doing the same things and expecting different results. It's too short to play the blame game or point fingers. Instead, learn to take responsibility for the part you played in letting yourself down, and make the decision to change it immediately.

Changing your life might mean seeking professional help, such as speaking to a psychiatrist or psychologist. They can help you unpack your painful trauma and provide you with tools to cope if that trauma resurfaces. Never feel embarrassed about seeking help when you can't find the answers on your own.

I've been in therapy on and off for many years, and I will continue to use it whenever I need to. Remember, life is a process. There's never a single moment where you "reach the mountaintop." Life is a continuous journey—so just enjoy the ride.

Life is like the changing of seasons—each one comes with its own set of challenges. It's not about whether troubles will come, because inevitably, trouble will come. It's about how you handle those challenges.

A therapist can help guide you through these seasons of life, providing you with lifelong tools that will become a permanent part of your personal toolbox for navigating difficulties.

Now, let me give you a warning: when you make the radical choice to change, people will start to fall away. You may no longer visit the same places or engage in the same activities. Your outlook on life will shift, and you'll begin to see people for who they really are and what they truly want from you.

Relationships will be lost—including some with family members—but don't

> "And once the storm is over, you won't remember how you made it through, how you managed to survive. You won't even be sure, in fact, whether the storm is over. But one thing is certain. When you come out of the storm, you won't be the same person who walked in."
> ~Haruki Murakami

turn back. If you do, people will never take you seriously. And what you left behind will still be waiting for you, only worse than before. Stay committed to your path.

"Although the world is full of suffering, it is also full of the overcoming of it."

-Helen Keller-

THE BIG F

> *The weak can never forgive. Forgiveness is the attribute of the strong.*
>
> *—Mahatma Gandhi*

Yes, I'm talking about the word *FORGIVENESS!* Forgiveness is an emotion that can be incredibly difficult to master. Holding onto unforgiveness means you are limiting your ability to experience true happiness, because it's impossible for two conflicting emotions to occupy your mind at the same time.

Forgiveness is a choice; a choice between remaining emotionally hostage to the past or moving forward toward a fulfilling life of happiness and wholeness.

Forgiveness is a conscious, deliberate decision to release feelings of resentment or vengeance toward a person or group who has harmed you, regardless of whether they deserve your forgiveness.

THE POWER OF Hell Naw!

"I never knew how strong I was until I had to forgive someone who wasn't sorry and accept an apology I never received."

~Author Unknown

Forgiving someone doesn't mean you accept or condone what they've done to hurt you. It simply means you are releasing the hold that the past has on you, allowing yourself to move forward. Forgiveness is more about freeing *you* than it is about them. It's not about letting them off the hook or excusing their actions. Some people even refer to forgiveness as a "selfish act" because it ultimately benefits *us* by freeing us from pain.

But forgiveness isn't just about forgiving others; it's also about forgiving *yourself*. Holding onto unforgiveness, whether toward yourself or others, is like giving your power away. It's as if you're throwing arrows at people, only for them to bounce back and harm you instead.

Forgiveness begins with taking responsibility. It requires reflecting on the role you played, what you allowed, and the boundaries you may have lacked. We are responsible for building the lives we want, which means we are also responsible for what we permit in or around us.

Additionally, we are responsible for how we respond to those who have hurt us. Setting boundaries is crucial—it helps limit the chances of being hurt again, empowering us to protect our peace and well-being.

Holding onto unforgiveness is like drinking poison and expecting the other person to die. It simply doesn't work, and it never will!

Being unforgiving of self and others can lead you to become:

- Angry

THE POWER OF *Hell Naw!*

- Resentful
- Bitter
- Vengeful
- Hostile
- Judgmental
- Lonely
- Fearful
- Joyless
- Defensive
- Exhausted
- Blaming
- Irrational
- Violent
- Manipulative
- Non-Communicative
- Self-Destructive
- Indifferent To Helpful Advice
- Emotionally Dead
- Untrusting
- Self-Absorbed
- Negative

- Cynical
- Self-Righteous
- Stubborn
- Hopeless
- Spiritually Bankrupt

Most people, me included, often think that when you forgive someone, you're helping *them*, not yourself.

But that's not true.

Many need to realize that forgiving someone doesn't just benefit the person who hurt you—it especially helps *you!*

https://www.thehopeline.com/

Here are 5 quick tips on the power of forgiveness.

1. **Release Yourself from the Past**: Forgiveness allows you to let go of the pain tied to past events, freeing your heart and mind from emotional burdens that hold you back.

THE POWER OF Hell Naw!

2. **Improves Mental and Physical Health**: Studies show that forgiveness can reduce stress, lower blood pressure, and even improve immune function, promoting overall well-being.

3. **Strengthen Relationships**: Forgiving others fosters empathy and understanding, paving the way for healthier, more resilient relationships.

4. **Boost Emotional Resilience**: Forgiveness builds inner strength, helping you to face future challenges with a positive, compassionate perspective.

5. **Embrace Inner Peace**: Letting go of resentment and anger allows peace to settle in, creating space for joy, gratitude, and personal growth.

Forgiveness isn't about excusing others' actions; it's about reclaiming your peace and empowering yourself to move forward.

"Forgiving is not forgetting; it's actually remembering—remembering and not using your right to hit back. It's a second chance for a new beginning."

-Desmond Tutu-

THE POWER OF *Hell Naw!*

DECLUTTER

VENUS CHANDLER

To de-clutter means to remove things you don't need from a space, making it more pleasant and useful. The same principle applies to people in your life. You need to remove those who don't add value to your life and your life's purpose. This isn't easy, and it might involve distancing yourself from relatives, close friends, children, jobs, or even parents.

De-cluttering your life is crucial because, without it, you won't be able to hear what God has for you. When your life is filled with chaos and confusion, everything becomes noisy, drowning out the guidance you need. If you can't hear God's instruction, you're like a lost child wandering in the wilderness.

I remember for years, everything around me was chaotic. Everyone I interacted with seemed to be in constant need or turmoil, and my life was filled with noise. I couldn't hear anything from God—no direction, no clarity, and no idea which way to turn. Deciding to de-clutter my life was the best decision I ever made.

THE POWER OF *Hell Naw!*

When I finally de-cluttered my life and could hear God's voice again, He guided me and revealed my purpose.

Before I understood my purpose, I made all kinds of decisions—financial, relationship, and otherwise. I spent time with platonic friends and with people who weren't aligned with my purpose, and because I didn't know what my purpose was, I accepted it.

I couldn't say, "*This doesn't fit into my purpose. This doesn't align with the design of my life. This isn't justification for my existence or the motivation that drives me.*"

I couldn't see that certain things didn't fit into the plan God had for me. So, I took on anything and everything. Even with dear friends, I didn't stop to ask myself, "*Is spending time with them at the present moment a part of my purpose?*"

I knew I needed to study. I knew I had a speaking engagement to prepare for. But before I understood all of this, I was open to anything and everything. And guess what? I got everything—the abusive guy, the job that didn't make me happy, and friends who betrayed me at every opportunity.

It was through those highs and lows that I discovered my purpose. My purpose in life wasn't to be a victim or to settle for second best. My purpose is to be the first choice, to always give my best, and to be seen as a woman of purpose, class, and substance. We've all let ourselves down at some point, but I knew I had to stop.

Now you understand why de-cluttering was so essential in my life, and I hope you can see why it's just as important for you.

In closing, the benefits of decluttering extend far beyond just tidying up our physical spaces—they bring clarity, peace, and a renewed sense of purpose to our lives. Decluttering creates room not only for our

THE POWER OF Hell Naw!

belongings to breathe but also for our minds and hearts to feel lighter and more at ease.

Each item we choose to let go of is a step toward freeing ourselves from unnecessary weight, reducing stress, and simplifying our environment. This process cultivates a sense of control and allows us to be more intentional about what we welcome into our lives, paving the way for joy and contentment.

With fewer distractions, our focus improves, and we gain a deeper connection to the present moment. Decluttering reminds us to prioritize what truly matters, helping us to cherish our possessions without letting them consume us.

As our surroundings become more organized, our inner world mirrors this transformation, bringing us closer to mental clarity, emotional balance, and a sense of fulfillment.

Ultimately, decluttering is a journey to rediscovering who we are and what we value. By creating physical and emotional space, we open ourselves to new opportunities, positive energy, and a simpler, more intentional life filled with purpose.

OWNING YOUR OWN *Crap!*

VENUS CHANDLER

A man may fail many times, but he isn't a failure until he begins to blame somebody else!

-J. Paul Getty

So, why do we blame others? Simple, it's easier. Blaming others allows us to avoid taking responsibility for our own mess. When we own our own mistakes, it means we must change, and change can be complex and difficult.

For years, I blamed everyone around me for my failures. Anyone who ever came into my life and hurt me-they were the ones at fault.

I never stopped to "own" my own issues because it was easier to point my finger at someone else. I didn't take responsibility for the choices I made, the friends I picked, the relationships I entered, the jobs I accepted, or the things I chose to participate in.

THE POWER OF *Hell Naw!*

I remember during my partying days, I prioritized going out, looking good, and staying out all night over being responsible—paying bills and taking care of my children. I would leave them home alone while I partied, and these reckless decisions cost me dearly. A single night of fun could lead to losing my job, my home, and even jeopardizing my kids' safety, with the state threatening to take them away.

One night in particular stands out. I was out with friends until the early morning, driving around, drinking, blasting music with a car full of people—and drugs. Meanwhile, my children were at home, asleep in their beds.

We got pulled over by the police, and I was told to get out of the car. The police conducted a search on both of us and the vehicle.

I was terrified.

But God intervened that night. One of the cops looked into my frightened eyes and told me to put my purse in the back seat and step out to be frisked by a female officer. The next thing I knew, I was being arrested—not for the drugs in my purse, but for an unpaid court ticket.

All I could think was, *"Oh no! My kids are home alone."*

As I was carted to jail, my mind kept racing—I knew my kids would be waking up soon, and I wouldn't be there. After being processed, I had to change into an orange jumpsuit, put on rubber slides, and was issued a cup, saucer, and an orange.

I cried the entire time.

Finally, after what felt like an eternity, I heard my name: *"Venus Chandler, pack up your things—you've been bailed out."*

I rushed home, and when I walked in, those sweet faces were looking up at me, confused and scared. You'd think after all of that, I would have straightened up and started owing to my mess, right?

No, I didn't.

Instead, I kept blaming everyone else. I told myself, *"The police were just messing with us because we were young and of color,"* or *"Why would they send*

THE POWER OF Hell Naw!

me to jail over something as small as an unpaid court ticket? They're just messing with me because I'm poor."

But my favorite excuse—the one I used most often—was, *"If I hadn't been messed up as a kid, I wouldn't be in this situation."*

That was my go-to line back then.

I had plenty of other excuses too. If I lost a job, I'd blame the company for not being flexible with their hours for single mothers. If I lost my home, I'd blame the landlord for not having empathy for a struggling single mom.

Years passed before I finally realized that blaming others wasn't fixing anything. I had to start owning my own choices. I had to dig deep and become aware of my responsibility for the poor decisions I made throughout my life.

Yes, my life started the way it did because the adults who were supposed to protect and guide me failed.

VENUS CHANDLER

But once I learned better, it became my responsibility to change the course of my own life.

In the end, I had to face the hard truth: no one was going to change my life for me. Blaming others may have provided temporary relief, but it didn't fix anything. It didn't heal the pain, rebuild what I lost, or moved me forward. Owning my decisions, both the good and the bad—was the turning point in my journey. Once I accepted responsibility, I was able to regain control of my life and my future.

Yes, my past shaped me, but it no longer defines me. I've learned that while I may not have been responsible for how my story began, I am fully responsible for how it ends. My mistakes don't define me, and neither do the people who hurt me. What defines me now is my strength, my resilience, and my decision to take charge of my own life.

As you reflect on your own life, I hope you realize the power in owning your choices. It's not always easy, but it's the only way to truly grow, heal, and move forward. You can rewrite your story, no matter how it began. And that, my friend, is where true freedom lies.

VENUS CHANDLER

NAVIGATING *Forward*

Now that we've explored the foundations of your power to confidently say, "Hell nah," it's time to focus on what moving forward truly looks like. Tools are only as effective as the way they are used. That's why this isn't just about handing you resources—it's about guiding you on how to use them to build a new and fulfilling life.

This book has been stirring within me since I released my very first book in 2018. Back then, sharing my story and truth came with a great deal of apprehension. But I knew there was more at stake than just my comfort. Saying "yes" to that journey wasn't just about my freedom—it was about creating a path for others, including you, to embrace self-empowerment.

With the heart of a coach, I took another step forward in 2019 by publishing a journal titled *Creating the New You*. It was a simple yet intentional writing tool, designed to give you the space to explore and navigate the process of becoming the best version of yourself.

THE POWER OF Hell Naw!

As I've grown and learned even more along this journey, I've been inspired to expand on that foundation by creating a comprehensive program to help you chart the course toward your transformation.

The main reason many people struggle to create a new life is that they lack a clear blueprint. It's similar to receiving a new desk or shelf that needs assembly—without instructions or a plan, you might end up placing screws in the wrong spots, throwing off the foundation. A desk leaning to one side wouldn't serve its purpose, and you wouldn't be able to get any work done. The same principle applies to life.

That's why I've created an exclusive program designed to help you reclaim your life and achieve new levels of success.

Through my experience, I've found that women in their mid-forties to late fifties often encounter unique challenges when striving to elevate their lives. These obstacles may arise from past decisions, difficult relationships, or the absence of healthy boundaries. Regardless of the cause, it's crucial to have a supportive, judgment-free space to rebuild and restore balance to your life.

This understanding led me to develop the program *Creating The New You.* This transformative program is built on seven foundational pillars designed to foster complete life success.

Those 7 pillars are:

1. Mindset
2. Physical & Nutritional Awareness
3. Relationships
4. Education
5. Home Ownership
6. Credit Building
7. Entrepreneurship

I firmly believe that these seven pillars have the power to transform a woman's life, making her truly unstoppable. Each pillar builds upon the others, and when understood and applied, a woman can position herself as an invaluable asset in any relationship she enters.

I have developed these seven pillars into a comprehensive, seven-part online program, where I serve as your coach, guiding you through each transformative aspect of your life. I am confident that if you fully embrace these pillars, you will unlock a life of freedom and fulfillment on multiple levels.

To join this empowering program, visit my website at https://kintsugitransformations.net. You'll gain the tools, insights, and clarity needed to piece together the missing elements of your life and elevate your relationships, as well as your personal and professional journey.

I look forward to seeing you on the other side—there is so much waiting for the *new you*!

Coach Venus

I will see you on the other side!!

ABOUT THE AUTHOR

VENUS CHANDLER

Venus, originally from Akron, Ohio, now resides in Los Angeles, California. She is a proud mother of three and grandmother to five.

With a professional career spanning 36 years in nursing, Venus has dedicated her life to serving others in various medical facilities, including Lynwood Healthcare Center, Los Angeles Community Hospital, and Bay Vista. She has spent the last nine years as a Nurse Manager at Lighthouse Healthcare Center.

Venus is a published, number 1 best-selling international author, speaker, life coach, and advocate for survivors of childhood trauma. In 2016, she discovered her true purpose—advocating for women and girls, helping them reclaim their power, purpose, and voice. Once she realized her destiny, she acted, committing herself to uplifting others.

Since then, Venus has embraced her calling, moving freely in the plan God has for her life. She launched her own business, *Kintsugi Transformations Life Coaching Services*, with the goal of helping women develop healthy minds, which she believes are essential for building strong, healthy communities.

Her motto: *"We are strength in numbers!"*

Venus is also the author of her autobiography, *A Silent Scream: My Story, My Truth*, in which she shares her journey of overcoming obstacles and

THE POWER OF Hell Naw!

pursuing her dreams. She is living proof that with determination, anyone can discover their purpose and achieve their goals, one step at a time.

VENUS CHANDLER

OTHER BOOKS BY THE AUTHOR

The darkness in her eye represents her past. The light in her eye represents her future. The tear on her face represents the pain she endured. The story represents her freedom and healing. Silent No More is an anthology about childhood trauma. The authors are women who experienced horrific abuse and mistreatment when they should have been protected & cherished. They were violated as minors. They were threatened to keep it secret and forced to keep quiet. Featuring Anjanette Robinson, Brandi Marsh, Carra Braxton, Danniel S. Withers, Jaynel Jones, LaLisa Morgan, Lucretia Y. Hayes, Melanie Rossum, Melissa McGill, Porshe Williams, Tanya DeFreitas, and Vernita Edwards, with a bonus by Terry Chandler. As adults, these women are reclaiming their liberty and victory by telling their truth and they are Silent No More! It's not an easy read, but it was not an easy journey getting to the place of being able to share what they experienced.

VENUS CHANDLER

The story within *A Silent Scream* is far from unique, yet it resonates with countless others who have walked a similar path. In writing this book, Venus Chandler brings attention to the often-overlooked struggles that many face daily. Themes of molestation, rape, addiction, money, and prostitution shaped her journey, but they do not define her. Venus is not a victim of her past; she is a survivor.

This book is written for every broken soul, especially for women who have endured unimaginable trials. It reaches out to those who have wrestled with thoughts of suicide, harbored anger, or dealt with the weight of PTSD. *A Silent Scream* is dedicated to anyone who has had their innocence stolen, suffered sexual abuse, or been harmed by those they trusted to protect them.

Venus Chandler invites readers to reclaim themselves and find their voice. In *A Silent Scream*, she extends permission to release the grip of the past. With each breath and each moment of hope, this book encourages readers to dream again and to become the person they have always longed to be.

THE POWER OF *Hell Naw!*

Courage.

This is what it takes to pick up the pieces of a shattered heart. Although challenging, these women took a fearless leap and answered the call. It was a call to healing, restoration and trust in God.

Walk with us beyond the echoes of a shattered heart onto the path of healing and redemption.

VENUS CHANDLER

Courage.

This is what it takes to pick up the pieces of a shattered heart. Although challenging, these women took a fearless leap and answered the call. It was a call to healing and restoration.

Join Coach Venus Chandler and four other courageous women who walk beyond the echoes of a shattered heart onto the path of healing and redemption.

THE POWER OF *Hell Naw!*

Writing is therapy, and Coach Venus is here to help you mend your healing heart through writing.

This journal is designed to accompany the book: SUDDENLY Single-An Anthology. Coach Venus compiled this journal in hopes that you will take your journey a step further by writing your pain and tears away.

Receive the healing your heart needs and watch breakthroughs come on the other side!

VENUS CHANDLER

Brutal Courage is an anthology about cruel strength and the women who possess it. In this book, you will follow the journey of 12 women who have experienced life-changing moments that reshaped their world forever. They had to be strong, courageous, and fearless.

It was often a matter of life or death. Their will to live was stronger than they were at times, and that helped them get through. Featuring Anthologist and Lead Author, Tanya DeFreitas, along with Anjanette Robinson, Audrea V. Heard, Barbara Thomas, Cheriese Foster, Jaynel Jones, Keci Monique, Lupe Duran, Melissa Brown, Melissa McGill, Savannah West, and Venus Chandler. They are bold, brave, and united as they join forces to tell their stories.

These are stories of tragedy & triumph, victimization & victory. The truth is revealed, secrets are exposed; It gets real, it gets raw, it gets BRUTAL!

www.ingramcontent.com/pod-product-compliance
Lightning Source LLC
Chambersburg PA
CBHW050657160426
43194CB00010B/1974